Extracts from the Authorized King James Version
of the Bible, the rights of which are vested in
the Crown in perpetuity within the United Kingdom,
are reproduced by Eyre & Spottiswoode Publishers,
Her Majesty's Printers, London.

The words are taken from:
Luke 1:5, 26, 27, 30-33, 38; 2:1, 3-5, 7-16, 18-20, 40
Matthew 2:1-3, 8, 9, 11-15, 19-21, 23

First published in the United States 1989
by Dial Books
A Division of Penguin Books USA Inc.
2 Park Avenue
New York, New York 10016

N
1   3   5   7   9   10   8   6   4   2

Library of Congress Cataloging in Publication Data
Brent, Isabelle.
The Christmas story.

Summary: King James Version of the Bible Christmas story
retold, accompanied by the illustrator's illuminations.
1. Brent, Isabelle. 2. Christmas in art.
1. Jesus Christ–Nativity. 2. Bible stories – N.T.
1. Title.
ND3410.B74A4 1989   745.6'7'0924   89-1149
ISBN 0-8037-0730-4

The full-color watercolor artwork was prepared with 24-carat gold leaf
applied by hand. It was then reproduced in five colors: the
watercolor art was separated in four-color process, with
the gold photographed separately and reproduced
as the fifth color in metallic gold ink.

The Christmas Story

from The King James Version

Illuminated by
·ISABELLE·BRENT·

Dial Books · New York

IN THE DAYS of Herod the King, the angel Gabriel was sent from God unto a city named Nazareth, to a virgin espoused to a man whose name was Joseph; and the virgin's name was Mary.

And the angel said, Thou shalt bring forth a son, and shalt call his name Jesus. He shall be called the Son of the Highest: and of his kingdom there shall be no end.

And Mary said, Behold the handmaid of the Lord. And the angel departed from her.

IT CAME to pass that there went out a decree that all the world should be taxed, every one in his own city. And Joseph went up from Nazareth to the city called Bethlehem, to be taxed with Mary his wife, being great with child.

AND SHE brought forth her firstborn son, and wrapped him in swaddling clothes, and laid him in a manger; because there was no room for them in the inn.

There were in the same country shepherds keeping watch over their flock by night. And the angel of the Lord came upon them, and they were sore afraid.

AND THE angel said unto them, Fear not: for behold, I bring you good tidings of great joy. For unto you is born a Saviour, which is Christ the Lord. And this shall be a sign unto you; ye shall find the babe wrapped in swaddling clothes, lying in a manger.

Suddenly there was a multitude of the heavenly host saying, Glory to God in the highest, and on earth peace, good will toward men.

The shepherds
said one to another,
Let us now go to Bethlehem.
And they found Mary and
Joseph, and the babe lying in
a manger.

And all they that heard it
wondered at those things
which were told them by the
shepherds. But Mary kept
all these things, and pondered
them in her heart.

And the shepherds returned,
praising God.

BEHOLD, there came wise men from the east, saying, Where is he that is born King of the Jews? For we have seen his star in the east, and are come to worship him.

WHEN HEROD the King heard these things, he was troubled. And he sent them to Bethlehem, and said, Go and search diligently for the child; and when ye have found him, bring me word again, that I may come and worship him also.

WHEN THEY

had heard the King, they departed; and lo, the star went before them, till it stood over where the young child was.

And they saw the young child with Mary his mother, and fell down and worshipped him; and when they had opened their treasures, they presented unto him gifts: gold, and frankincense, and myrrh.

Being warned in a dream that they should not return to Herod, they departed into their own country another way.

AND THE angel appeared to Joseph in a dream, saying, Arise, and take the child and his mother, and flee into Egypt, for Herod will seek the child to destroy him.

When he arose, he took the child and his mother by night, and departed into Egypt, and was there until the death of Herod.

BUT WHEN Herod was dead, an angel appeared in a dream to Joseph in Egypt, saying, Take the child and his mother, and go into the land of Israel: for they are dead which sought the young child's life.

And he took the child and his mother, and came into the land of Israel, and dwelt in Nazareth.

AND THE

child grew, and waxed strong in spirit, filled with wisdom: and the grace of God was upon him.

CHESTERFIELD COUNTY LIBRARY
CLOVER HILL